The Chunky Method Handbook

Your Step-by-Step Guide to Write That Book Even When Life Gets in the Way

ALLIE PLEITER

Cover art by Sara Roney and Sunrise Studios

PRINT ISBN-10: 0-9972982-0-0
PRINT ISBN-13: 978-0-9972982-0-8

CONTENTS

CHAPTER ONE: THE WRITING LIFE

"I've always wanted to write a book."
"I've got a book started that I never finished."
"How on earth do you find time to write?"
"Why am I always struggling like crazy to meet my deadline?"

I hear these kinds of statements all the time. People find out I'm a working writer, and they picture me sitting peacefully in a beautiful library, pondering volumes of classic literature, sipping tea, bursting with inspiration.

Eh...not so much.

There are days where my life feels close to that—minus the tea (I'm a die-hard coffee drinker), minus the library (you'll learn more about where I write later), and often minus the inspiration. Like almost every writer I know, if I waited for inspiration to strike I'd never finish a chapter, much less a book.

The truth of the matter is that I don't find time to write, I make time to write. Finding time implies that inspiration is sitting there like a penny on the sidewalk, waiting to be grasped. There are loads of things grasping at my time, from packed days to stacked piles on my desk. If I'm going to write, I've got to make the time to make it happen.

I started my professional life in the not-for-profit world, writing grant proposals. It meant juggling multiple projects simultaneously, adhering to deadlines, and working without many resources—good training for a novelist, even if I didn't realize it at the time. To cope with the demands, I began studying time management strategies and productivity tactics. When I made the shift from fundraising and nonprofit to fiction and nonfiction, I realized that with a little tweaking, many of the same principles I had learned to get my grants delivered on time applied to the creative process. Suddenly the idea of breaking down the large task of writing a novel into reasonable, scheduled, tailored-to-my-speed "chunks" made the process much more manageable. Writing my books became infinitely less stressful, yet not one bit less exciting or artistic. The Chunky Method was born. I began sharing my ideas with fellow writers, who found them useful, motivating, and downright practical.

After all, creative work is still work. It's pleasant work, but if you dream of making your living writing—or maybe just finally typing those magic words "THE END" on that novel—you're going to have to figure out how to get the job done. In the time you've got, with the life you live.

The answer isn't that you need more talent or new inspiration or, sorry to say, that spiffy new laptop you've been eying. Those are tools, and tools are good, but only if you have a strategy for using them to your best advantage. By the end of this book, you'll have a system that would even work with tools as simple as index cards!

I have been teaching the Chunky Method in workshops and seminars for years, and it never stops being a terrific thrill for me. Watching a writer unlock the strengths of his or her natural style is like watching lightning strike. Hearing how so many writers have increased their productivity in ways they never thought possible—without stressing out or strangling their creative voice—well, that's music to my ears. Writers often come up to me after one of my Chunky seminars and tell me how delighted they are to discover they can dependably, predictably write no matter what their style. They are relieved to know their craving to crawl inside a closet and not come out for hours doesn't indicate some sort of mental instability. They're thrilled to know their short attention span in writing doesn't spell artistic doom. They're less stressed and more excited because they now have a practical and adaptable path to reaching their goals. I hope this book will do the same for you.

So how will the Chunky Method unlock this same path for you? If you're looking for a magic bullet or easy formula, I'm sorry to disappoint you. I suspect most of this book will feel like creative common sense to you, because that's what it is. You'll learn how to create a system based on your needs that breaks the enormous job of writing a book down into daily or weekly tasks—because that's how it gets done.

Are you ready? Let's get Chunky!

YOUR MUSE VS. YOUR DEADLINE

Deadlines are part of every working writer's life. Unless you are seeking to publish something that's already written, you have a deadline. And even then, you may have a revision deadline. Deadlines are crucial to how our business works, so if you can't work toward a deadline, you're essentially a hobby-writer. Don't get me wrong; I don't look down on hobby-writers. You're the catch-and-release fishermen of our profession, doing it all for the sheer pleasure of the experience.

I doubt you're reading this book because the pleasure of the experience has been carrying you away on clouds of productive bliss. You're reading it because you want to figure out how make this thing called writing work in the real world—the one with needy kids and pushy bosses and bathrooms that need cleaning and grass that needs cutting.

The one with writer's block.

It's you against the goal, your muse vs. your deadline. Writers' Fight Club. And for me, the first rule of Writers' Fight Club is that you absolutely talk about Writers' Fight Club. You face the problem head on, force your muse to read your game plan (even if you have to first figure out what that game plan is—and don't worry, I'll help with that), and get your creative self cooperating with your practical self.

If writing were like manufacturing, it wouldn't be hard to know that wheel A goes into cog B on day C. You could line up tasks on a timeline and plot your way from chapter 1 to the epilogue. The trouble is, we've convinced ourselves writing can't be held to schedules and processes like manufacturing when, in fact, it can. I absolutely, positively believe it can. If we can train squirrels to waterski (go ahead, Google it), you can train your muse to read a schedule.

I'm not saying there won't be days when the words fly from your fingers and you watch the pages fill in sheer glee. Those days are the reason we all write. Those days just can't be the only days you write. You may think of your muse as a temperamental diva, dangling brilliance just out of your reach, but if you conduct the exercises in this book, you'll discover she can be a reasonable gal. Properly harnessed to respect a deadline, your muse can become a dependable asset, a resource your employer can respect and someone with whom your family can actually stand to share a house.

A well-harnessed muse is the mark of a professional. Come along with me and let's find yours.

MANAGEMENT MATTERS

"But it's art. It's the creative process. You can't cram it into a system or it'll wither and die."

I hear that all the time.

Nonsense.

Your muse, your talent, is just that: yours. It is an asset, not an opponent. Don't believe the myth that you can whip up a cooperative muse just because you receive a contract. It's not an add-contract-and-stir recipe. Your ability to manage your muse matters whether you are currently published or seeking publication.

If you're reading this book because you've just inked your signature on a spiffy new book contract or digital packaging program—congratulations! You need to learn the Chunky Method because the next year will ask things of you that you never imagined. If you haven't yet signed a contract or launched a digital deal—extra special congratulations! You've come to the smart conclusion that you ought to get a working system in place before you need it. The bottom-line is that if you want to write, you need to learn how to get writing done, how to make writing happen.

Picture yourself accepting an offer or pushing "send" on your upload. Think about what it will feel like to say "yes" to the deal to write your first book. Or your next book. Or your next really big book. The reality is that in this business, that delightful "yes" is very quickly followed by a demanding "when?"

"When can you have the revised manuscript to us?"

"When can you take this proposal and have it fully finished?"
"When will you have your next book ready?"

Publishers—even independent and digital self-publishers—all work on production schedules. Can you? You don't want to pull the answer to that "when?" question out of the sky—too much of your career is riding on it.

Even if signing traditional publishing contracts isn't in your career plans, there are other considerations. Many agents, for example, don't want to consider aspiring writers until they've finished their manuscripts. Most publishing houses won't look at a debut manuscript unless it's complete. And you can't upload for sale what you haven't finished. So, we all have deadlines—some of us just haven't realized it yet. If you want to grow and progress as a writer, you've got to know how to get from wherever you are to "THE END" in a reasonable, practical, predictable way.

What's more, you want to be able to do that within the context of your real life—even while you may be planning for your daughter's wedding, a vacation, a move across the country—and that's just the stuff you know is coming! If you can create a productive system for your writing, you are in much better shape to cope when the unexpected happens. Writers using the

Chunky Method can calmly adapt when the hard drive crashes, when your wife tells you she's been offered that job in Fiji (lucky you!), or when your appendix decides to act up. With the Chunky Method, writers can both see a squeeze coming and make adjustments in the midst of one.

The world is filled with talented writers. Talent is good—essential, even. But writers who can get the job done, who can deliver on a deadline, and who are less likely to pitch a fit of panic at the last minute—those are the writers in demand, the ones everyone wants to work with. Master the elements of the Chunky Method, and you're well on your way to professionalism and salability.

CAN CREATIVITY REALLY BE MANAGED?

Maybe you've gotten this far and are thinking, "my muse isn't likely to be cooperative." You've spent too many hours staring at that blinking cursor or that blank page, wondering how all those wonderful ideas that accosted you in the shower disappeared once you finally made it to the keyboard. You're convinced creativity is a fickle thing, unmanageable and uncontainable.

Some of history's greatest writers would take issue with that. Many write at the same time, in the same place, or for a certain amount of hours or pages every working day. Sure, there's a whole mystique around the idea of "hiding in a cabin in the woods to write the Great American Novel," but it's mostly smoke and mirrors. Working writers are just that; working consistently, productively. Why can't that be you?

Creativity can be a habit. It can be trained to follow a schedule and to respect a deadline. Your brain, after all, is your creative muscle, and muscles respond to training. The Chunky Method is, at its core, a training schedule. If you take the time to identify how your creativity works and make plans based on that information, you'll tame your wild muse.

While you're feeling inspired, take a moment to write down what you think you would gain by training that wild muse of yours. What stresses would you lose? What gains would productivity bring you? What larger goal would finishing that manuscript bring you? Is it a financial goal or a personal one? Is it the sense of accomplishment? Something as simple as the knowledge that you are capable of writing a whole book? Being less of a "wild card" in the context of your family? Think about what success would look like to you, and write down three reasons why being more consistently productive will improve your writing life. Get as specific and vivid as you can so it can set fire to your motivation!

Being consistently productive will help me by:

1)_____

_____

_____

2)_____

_____

_____

3)_____

_____

_____

CHAPTER TWO: THE AMAZING CHUNKY METHOD

Allow me to introduce you to the amazing Chunky Method. After such a build up, you may be expecting a complex concept. It's not.

Ask yourself: How much quality writing can you get done in a single sitting if not interrupted? If I were to give you an environment of your choice with the equipment of your choice and stood guard at the door, how many words could you write before the words stopped coming? That amount is your chunk. It's that simple.

It is so simple because most of us have a consistent chunk. We like to think that our muse comes and goes, that some days the words will gush out of us in great torrents and other days it will be like scraping bits of our soul off the sidewalk. Okay, some days it is just like that (we're artistic personalities, after all, and that stereotype didn't evolve out of nowhere). The surprising truth is that *only some days* are like that. Most days, were I to put you in the situation I just described, you would produce close to the same amount of words. Really. Your chunk is unique to you, but it is a remarkably consistent thing. It can be flexible, it can even be altered (more on that later), but it is consistent enough to be the basis of some very effective planning. It might even be the key to your success.

Before you sit back in your chair and cross your arms over your chest in disbelief, allow me to prove my point. Let's go find your chunk. Because when we do, all kinds of great things can happen.

FIGURING OUT YOUR CHUNK

Now that you know what a chunk is and what it can do, how do you figure out what yours is? Don't panic, but it will involve a small bit of math. Yes, I know you're a words person, and the thought of bringing a calculator along on your journey makes you nervous, but trust me—it won't be much.

As explained above, your chunk is the amount of *quality* writing you can get done in a single sitting if not interrupted. You could sit down and write "I am writing" for two hours and fill a notepad or a computer file, but it's not about the physical act of putting words down. Your chunk reflects how much your creativity can produce before it runs out of juice. How long your ideas can flow before they peter out. They do peter out at some point, for all of us. We can be chugging along at a satisfying speed and then "poof" we've used up our imagination for the time being.

The important thing to remember here is that such a point is *not* writer's block. It's simply the end of your chunk. You haven't run out of ideas, you've just run out of them *for the time being*. Like being full after a meal or running out of gas in your car. It's not a disaster or a crisis of identity, it's just a function of your capacity. Accept it, wield it like the tool it is, and you become far more productive.

EXPLORE YOUR CHUNKINESS

Let's get down to business and identify your chunk.

Make plans to sit down and write until you run out of steam. You may have a sense of how much time that might be, or you may have no idea. That's okay; you'll know by the end of our experiment. Start now.

The number of words I wrote was:
_____

You're not done. We need to be a little more scientific than that. Do it again five times, on five different days, so that you have five different instances of writing to the end of your creativity. Write them here, putting your number from above in the first slot:

Session	Date	# of Words
#1		
#2		
#3		
#4		
#5		

If you're like most people, the number of words in each of the instances will be surprisingly similar. That's the great secret of the Chunky Method; our muse is more consistent than we ever give her credit for. In fact, I believe she's just itching to prove her reliability.

If you've never devoted serious time to your writing before, the numbers you see above may surprise you. If you've been getting serious about your writing, you may have been able to make a general prediction about your chunk from experience.

Now for the math (take a deep breath if necessary):

Total all the words in writing sessions 1-5	
Divide that number by 5	

If you remember your third grade math, this gives you the average of all your five experimental sessions. Round up (or down) to a nice basic number, and that's your chunk. Write that here:

```
My CHUNK is _____ words.
```

Here's an example:

Back when I first started writing, my chunk was about 600 words. It's much higher than that now (more on how that happened later), but with two small kids in tow and not a lot of experience, 600 words was all I could pound out. Here's how my worksheet looked:

Word count Session 1:	540
Word count Session 2:	635
Word count Session 3:	590
Word count Session 4:	650
Word count Session 5:	550
Word count total:	2,965
Divided by 5 =	593

My Chunk was 600 words.

That was my chunk, and now you know yours. So how do you use that knowledge?

It starts by identifying if you're a BIG chunk writer, or a SMALL chunk writer. If you have a day job or something else that keeps you from writing full time, I place the dividing line between big and small chunk writers at 1,000 words. That means that if your chunk is less that 1,000 words, chances are you're a small chunk writer. Conversely, if your chunk is more than 1,000 words, you're likely a big chunk writer.

If you're a working writer—meaning that your main daily occupation is writing, whether or not you are drawing a paycheck—then I estimate the line between big chunk and small chunk hits at around 2,000 words.

BIG CHUNK WRITERS

So, what does it mean to be a big chunk writer? Big chunk writers are the "dive deep" writers, the ones who must totally immerse themselves in the story to make progress. Their work demands a certain set of circumstances to be satisfying, and they often aren't fond of multi-tasking. What does that mean for their writing? You most likely are a big chunk writer if:

1. You need a dedicated space to write.
You aren't likely to be happy banging out your chapters at the dining room table. You need someplace where you can "hide away" from life's noise and distractions—preferably with a door that shuts (and maybe locks!). Writing works best for you in a place you can call your own.

2. Your writing is affected by your environment. Much like the space, you probably require certain things around you when you write. It might be silence, it might be a certain kind of music. You care about your desk, what's on the walls, your chair, your keyboard and monitor because you plan on spending a lot of extended time in this space. A shared, messy, or a make-do office will irritate you and make you feel like you don't have what you need to be creative.

3. You write for extended periods or not at all. It's hard for you to do the writing equivalent of "a cat nap" because you need a big block of time to find your rhythm while writing. Unless you're writing full time (and maybe even if you are), it's hard to carve out the multiple uninterrupted hours you need to be at your creative best. You're likely to find a daily goal frustrating to keep because chances are you can't find a large enough span of time every day.

4. The "Cabin in the Woods" appeals to you. Hiding yourself away in a cabin in the woods to finish your novel sounds like heaven to the big chunk writer. There's so much you could do if you could just be left alone long enough! Solitude feeds your rhythm, seclusion is one way to ignite your muse. You'd love a writing retreat or a month alone with your laptop at a beach house.

5. Ergonomics matter to you. Spending extended hours in one chair means that unless you want a bad back, you need to make sure it's a good chair. Big chunk writers often battle carpel tunnel syndrome, neck and shoulder issues, and other physical ailments that attack the writer's primary tool: himself. You need to invest the time and money to ensure your support system—chair, desk, keyboard, mouse, monitor, lighting, etc.—helps your body rather than hurts it.

LITTLE CHUNK WRITERS

Little chunk writers have a different style. They tend to be more flexible, adaptable…and, well, distractable. They take life—and writing—in smaller bites and often juggle multiple projects. What does that mean for our study of chunkiness? You are most likely a little chunk writer if:

1. You can write anytime, anywhere. It doesn't matter where you are—at coffee bars, on park benches, in libraries, on the airplane—nothing seems to distract you from writing. This sounds like a good thing—and it is—but it can also lead to an "I'll squeeze it in somewhere" attitude that makes it hard to devote time to writing.

2. You easily tune out distractions. If you can tune out *SpongeBob SquarePants* while finishing Chapter 3, you have a big advantage when it comes to productivity. You don't need the right environment, pleasing music (or silence), or lots of visual cues to spark your muse. You can crawl inside a project regardless of external circumstances.

3. You write often. Flexibility in time and place means little chunk writers can fit writing around and into a busy life. A daily word count—albeit smaller—is highly possible for you. This also means cramming for a deadline is more difficult because you're not accustomed to long stretches of writing.

4. Any tools will do. You can write on or with just about anything because long writing timeframes are not a factor. Tablets, notepads, laptops, even index cards and cell phones can be adapted to hold the small batches of words that make up your chunk. Ergonomics don't make much difference, which can free up a lot of possibilities.

COMBO-CHUNK WRITERS
What if you're a little bit of each?

Most of us have some of the behaviors of big chunk and little chunk writers, but certain situations call for a true mix of the styles. I call these people combo-chunk writers, because productivity in their environments requires a deliberate blending of both kinds of Chunky behavior. These are usually people whose time constraints fluctuate in regular ways, such as:

- Parents with small children or children needy in other ways
- Teachers
- Writers with full-time day jobs

Each of these writers has (hopefully) somewhat predictable times where they have big chunks available to them, and other times where they have small chunks. The fluctuation doesn't matter much, just the awareness of it. Teachers, for example, have to be small chunk writers during the school year but can be big chunk writers on their summers off. Active parents or the full-time employed may think of themselves as big chunk writers on the weekends, but may discover they have the capacity to be a small chunk writer during the week.

The trick is to identify what you would gain by adding "the other side." If you work full time, for example, you might only think you can get writing done on the weekends. What if you were to explore your small chunk side during the week, filling an index card with 200 words every night on the train home? You'd add an extra big chunk every week before you even hit Saturday's cup of coffee, not to mention the additional push your imagination has been given by dipping your toes into your manuscript all week long.

Look at your week—we'll talk more about the practicalities of how to do that in Chapter 5— and see where your Chunky capacities lie. With a little planning, you'll be able to wield your personal style to its maximum productivity.

THE CHUNKY TRUTH

We need to stop right here and declare one important truth:

Big chunk and little chunk writers are equals.

One is not more saleable than the other. One is not more dedicated than the other. One is not more talented than the other. They are equally capable of producing great work.

Little chunk writer that I am, for years I felt myself inferior to all those people who locked themselves away on writers' retreats for days on end. Surely those folks who wrote non-stop for hours, who stayed up all night, who met their deadlines in a caffeine-crazed flurry of typing were more committed to their craft than I was. I was too steadily productive to be a "real artist."

I couldn't have been more wrong.

The truth is that I work as hard as the next novelist—I just don't work as *long* in a single sitting as the next novelist. This can help inform tone and style. For me, my short chunks help lend a lightness and a sparkle to my work that would vanish if I tried to pound out a longer text in one sitting.

I hope you hear what I'm saying: You can be productive and professional no matter what your personal writing style. Writers of any size chunk can learn to develop a professional, consistent output and reach their goals.

You know your chunk—embrace it! Get ready to utilize it! You don't have to stand up wherever you are, right now, and declare "I'm a big chunk writer!" Or "I'm a little chunk writer!" But you could. I would applaud you if you did.

CHAPTER THREE: USING YOUR CHUNK

Now you know the size of your chunk, and what that means for how you work. That's useful information, but it's only half of the Chunky Method's power. The real strength of chunkiness lies in its ability to predict and improve how you work toward a deadline.

Whenever you write, you owe it to yourself to give yourself a deadline if a publisher hasn't already done you that favor. Goals are powerful things. Goals make action happen, prevent sidetracks, and motivate us for long-term tasks (like writing a book). Face it; if this were easy, I wouldn't hear *"I've been meaning to write a book, but...*" as much as I do. I've heard it said that only twenty percent of the people who start a book make it to typing those two magic words "THE END." If you want to be in that top twentieth percentile who get the job done, the Chunky Method is here to help.

Take a deep breath; this is going to require some additional math, but I promise it will be worth it.

WHAT'S WORTH COUNTING?

Back in 1997, when I started writing, nearly everything was measured by page count. Contracts required books of a certain number of pages, book formats were measured by pages, contests required a certain number of pages.

The digitized world of laptops, word processors, e-books and e-readers has changed the measuring stick. Nearly every publisher, most contests, almost every contract, and most working writers I know see the world in word count now. The days where life was measured in "Courier 12pt. double-spaced with one-inch margins"—which universally counted as 250 words per page—have gone away.

Publishing industry standards aside, Chunky writers measure in word count because it's a smaller increment. This makes it easier to adapt, and can give us a more useful tool for both big chunk and small chunk writers because chunks can come in more sizes.

Go ahead and open your word processing program of choice. Nearly every one available today has the capacity to measure word count. Some of them even display it for you while you're writing (that's good, you want that, even if it feels like too much pressure right now). If not, take a moment and measure how many words fit on your screen display at any given moment. This is especially useful if you work on a portable device like an iPad, AlphaSmart, or even your smart-phone. However you arrive at the measurement, make sure you have a reliable, easily accessible way to count your words whenever you sit down to write.

Once you've got that, you're ready to move ahead.

THE CHUNKY METHOD WRITING PLAN

The Chunky Method's writing plan answers one—maybe *the*—vital question:

How do I get from chunk to book?

Just as with steps on a staircase, with the Chunky Method, you go one step at a time to reach your goal of the next level. With the Chunky Method writing plan, you calculate how many chunks of writing it will take to reach the end of your first draft.

That's a simple question with a complex answer. You'd be amazed, however, how many writers refuse to ask themselves the question. They resist chopping their work up into manageable segments, thinking it will hobble their muse. After all, making a plan turns it into work—and this is *art*, not work.

You already know how I feel about that particular myth.

In the following sections I'll show you a clear, stress-reducing system to map your path to completion. Follow this formula, and you should find yourself typing "THE END" exactly when you plan to or need to without too many surprises.

Step 1: How large is your target manuscript?

As the old saying goes, start with the end in mind. The categories are a little more fluid in these electronic book days, and lengths vary dramatically. If you need somewhere to start, here are the range of accepted word counts in the most basic genres (total word count by words):

Single title books (any genre)	85,000 - 100,000
Novellas	20,000 - 40,000
Short genre fiction/ series novels	45,000 - 65,000
Mysteries	55,000 - 75,000
Young adult novel	60,000 - 80,000
Sci-fi/fantasy	80,000 - 140,000

Of course, these are generalizations, and as such, they continually change. If you know exactly which publisher you are targeting, most houses publish their preferred word count along with their other submission guidelines. If you are seeking to write a nonfiction book, these numbers might not reflect your specific project.

It's in your best interest to make an educated guess and give yourself a sensible target. You need a total word count on which to base your Chunky formula.

Write the target word count of your manuscript here:

Now, let's talk about how to use this important number. For the purposes of explanation, we're going to use a nice round figure for our target word count: 100,000 words.

Step 2: Planned over-writing

Stephen King, along with myself and many other working writers I know, plans for the first draft of his manuscript to be about 10% over the required word count. Write too far under, and you're likely to revert to adding unneeded filler, spending too much time in description, or keeping scenes which don't accomplish much. Trust me, padding a manuscript under deadline is no fun at all and doesn't result in clean, tight writing.

If you go too far over, you'll find yourself in the painful, unenviable position of needing to quickly axe large chunks of your manuscript. This, in my opinion, is the only thing more unpleasant than needing to stuff in extra words. Hacking them out never feels like pruning—it always feels like oral surgery. Don't hand yourself such an excruciating problem!

Here's an added bonus to planned over-writing: grace. There are days where I look at my accomplished chunk and think, *"Well, that's part of the doomed 10% for sure."* Think of it as creative margin—you know you've got a few words to spare, so the pressure to make every first-draft word sparkling and perfect eases up. I've found a little grace in the form of planned overwriting goes a long way toward boosting productivity. It doesn't have to be perfect, it just has to be written.

> For yourself, take the word count you wrote above and multiply it by 1.1, rounding it up to a nice even number:
>
> _____

Using our explanation target of 100,000 words, our target will now be increased to 110,000. With me so far? Good, because now it gets to the real fun.

Step 3: Divide by your Chunk.

There's an old joke *"How do you eat an elephant? One bite at a time."* That's a silly example of how to apply the Chunky concept to your manuscript, but it utilizes the powerful truth that you don't have to write the whole thing right now, just the current chunk of it. It sounds simplistic, but you'll be amazed how energizing and empowering this smaller goal can be. And yes, it requires math, but not too much.

1. Your 110% word count:	
2. What you've established as your chunk:	
3. Divide line 1 by line 2:	

Line three tells you how many chunks it will take you to type those magic words "THE END" on the first draft of your manuscript.

Just for clarification, I'll work this math on our example:

1. Example 110% word count:	110,000
2. Example chunk:	600 words
3. 110,000 divided by 600	183.33 or roughly 184 chunks

This tells us that it will take 184 chunks to reach the end of our example manuscript. The path from here to "THE END" is 184 chunks—that's news you can use! The next section will show you how.

HOW MANY CHUNKS IN YOUR WEEK?

You may think the key to productivity is how many words you can write. It is, in some ways—but that's hardly the whole story. If we wrote in a perfect world where nothing else competed for our time, it would be.

We don't live in a perfect world.

As a matter of fact, most of us are struggling to get the words down on paper in a highly imperfect world, one that seems at odds with our writing wishes.

As such, they key here is not so much how *many* words, but how *often* you write them. Once you get accustomed to the Chunky Method, you'll discover that one of the key markers is how often you get to your chunks.

In plain terms: how often a week do you write? This question helps you take the Chunky path you created in the last section and give it a home in the real world.

> Right now, I write _____ times per week.

I never find it helpful to think in terms of every day, because days are rarely the same. Adjusting our thinking to plot in terms of weeks gives us a little wiggle room for the real world to poke its nose in our business—and if your life is like mine, that happens all too often.

Back to our example:

Our example writer—we'll call her Wendy Writer for the moment—has a lot of demands on her time, so:

- If Wendy gets 1 chunk per week it will take Wendy 184 weeks to write her first draft. That's over three and a half years.
- If Wendy gets 2 chunks per week, it will take her 92 weeks, or just under two years.
- If Wendy gets 3 chunks per week, it will take 62 weeks—just over a year.
- If Wendy gets 4 chunks per week, she can finish her draft in 46 weeks—just under a year.

Obvious, right? Yes, and no. It could take Wendy over three years to write that book. I chose Wendy's stats as an example because I *was* Wendy. I had small children at home and could only manage one session of writing per week that produced about 600 words. I spent a lot of time beating myself up for how long it took me, but I needn't have given myself so much grief. The realities of my world made those numbers a fact. Facts are much better off faced than ignored. So let's look at yours right now:

1. The number of chunks needed to finish my first draft:	
2. The numbers of chunks per week I can write:	
3. Line 1 divided by Line 2 = the number of weeks it will take me to write my first draft:	
4. Optional—translate to months or years:	

If you don't like what you see above, don't worry, this isn't the end of the process—it's only the beginning. You can't chart a new path, however, until you know where your current one leads. Stick with me, because I promise you that even if you don't like the writing speed you just calculated, it is about to become your best writing partner.

MAKING A CHUNKY METHOD PLAN

Now you know how many weeks it currently takes you to write your manuscript—in a perfect world where nothing pulls you off track. If you live in a world like that, count yourself fortunate, because not many of us do. Writers often write themselves into logistical corners because they ignore the fact that life is very talented at getting in the way of our work.

Chunky writers arm themselves against this reality. Chunky writers look ahead, scope out the danger zones, and plan around them. No one wants to be the writer hounded by a vicious deadline, losing sleep and showers while the rest of their friends and family watch a crazed, caffeine-soaked dash to the finish line. It doesn't result in nice companions, or even good work.

It doesn't take massive organizational skills to help yourself cope with your writing demands. All it takes is a simple plan, one that can be accomplished on a single sheet of paper or a small spreadsheet. Let's take a look at another example.

Andy Author has a chunk of 600 words just like our previous writer, Wendy. Andy, however, works part time, so he currently can manage four chunks a week. This means he can think in terms of weekly word count as well as chunks. Since his four chunks of 600 words total him 2,400 weekly words, he's on track to finish his manuscript in 46 weeks. When he plots this out on a table, it looks something like this:

Week		Cum. Words	Week		Cum. Words	Week		Cum. Words
1		2,400	6		14,400	11		26,400
2		4,800	7		16,800	12		28,800
3		7,200	8		19,200	13		31,200
4		9,600	9		21,600	14		33,600
5		12,000	10		24,000	15		36,000

16		38,400	26		62,400	37		88,800
17		40,800	27		64,800	38		91,200
18		43,200	28		67,200	39		93,600
19		45,600	29		69,600	40		96,000
20		48,000	30		72,000	41		98,400
21		50,400	31		74,400	42		100,800
22		52,800	32		76,800	43		103,200
23		55,200	33		79,200	44		105,600
24		57,600	34		81,600	45		108,000
25		60,000	35		84,000	46		110,400

When laid out like this, some wonderful things happen. First, Andy is looking at smaller, weekly goals—and those always feel more doable. Yes, the final result is a 110,000 word manuscript, but that can be a daunting target. It's much more empowering to be shooting for his 2,400 weekly word count for 46 weeks. Goals that feel "doable" are always more likely to result in success.

Secondly, some natural benchmarks show up. Andy can look forward to hitting the vital first 10,000 words (enough to furnish sample chapters in a proposal) around Week 4—that's an excellent first benchmark to celebrate one month into his Chunky plan. Personally, I know I never really fall in love with a book until around the 20,000 word mark, and I know my best research questions—about the location, the occupations of my characters, cultures, and time periods for historical novels—come up around 30,000 words. It is useful, even critical, to know where on a calendar these needs and stops occur. I know it's best to plan my on-site research trips for around week 13 of my Chunky writing plan.

It's practical to translate these numbered weeks to actual months, but since every author will begin the process in different months of the year, its best to keep things in week numbers here and let you translate them into actual dates on your own.

Andy Author is a fictional guy, but he can teach us a real world lesson: We write in the real world, where real obstacles happen. So while this first chart is empowering and useful, it isn't realistic. Smart Chunky writers know that there will always be weeks where they cannot write at full speed. Vacations, family events, holidays—all these have an impact on our productivity. Workers in more traditional jobs plan for these things, and so should you.

Before Andy declares his deadline to be met in Week 46, he needs to insert some padding into the weeks where other things will command his time. Of course, not every obstacle gives us advance notice. Life can blindside you without warning. All the more reason to plan for the things you *do* know in advance.

Taking one vacation, one family event, and one holiday week into account, let's revisit Andy's Chunky Method writing plan:

Week		Cum. Words	Week		Cum. Words	Week		Cum. Words
1		2,400	7		14,400	13		28,800
2		4,800	8		16,800	14		31,200
3		7,200	9		19,200	15		33,600
4		9,600	10		21,600	16		36,000
5		12,000	11		24,000	17	X	36,000
6	X	12,000	12		26,400	18		38,400

19		40,800	30		67,200	41		91,200
20		43,200	31		69,600	42		93,600
21		45,600	32		72,000	43		96,000
22		48,000	33		74,400	44		98,400
23		50,400	34		76,800	45		100,800
24		52,800	35	X	76,800	46		103,200
25		55,200	36		79,200	47		105,600
26		57,600	37		81,600	48		108,000
27		60,000	38		84,000	49		110,400
28		62,400	39		86,400			
29		64,800	40		88,800			

Andy has added the special events into weeks 6, 17, and 35—the x's marked in the table. Note that the word count does not advance in those weeks. The end result is that the plan is extended to 49 weeks. This is a writing schedule for the real world, not just Andy's ideal writing environment. With this schedule, he is less likely to get frustrated, less likely to fall behind schedule, and less likely to encounter discouragement. Andy is in control. Each week, he has a ready benchmark to celebrate that he is on track, or to know he needs step it up so he can stay on course for completion on Week 49.

Andy will be more productive on this schedule. His friends, boss, and family will likely be happier with this schedule. And, if he's working under contract, his editor will be happy to know he's taken some contingencies into account. An author who can consistently meet deadlines is a pleasure to work with—don't you want to be that author?

WHAT IF YOUR CHUNK NEEDS TO CHANGE?

What if you took one look at the table on page forty and thought: "I don't like that. I want to write faster. I don't want to wait a year before I type 'THE END'?" What do you do then?

The good news is that the Chunky Method is not only a good planning tool, it's a good productivity improvement tool. Using the Chunky Method, I've increased my writing productivity 300% over the course of my career—not all at once, mind you, but in smart increments driven by the mathematical power of the Chunky Method. The same is possible for you, because you now have solid, individualized data to help you improve.

Let me use Andy's example to show you how.

The goal here is a universal one: write faster. Only a command like that isn't enough to get results. Exactly *how* can Andy write faster? The key is in the chunk. Andy can make small adaptations to his chunk and discover big results.

For example, watch what happens if we take Andy's plan from earlier and increase his chunk by only 50 words. That's not much more than the previous paragraph—a highly doable improvement.

Week		Cum. Words	Week		Cum. Words	Week		Cum. Words
1		2,600	6	X	13,000	11		26,000
2		5,200	7		15,600	12		28,600
3		7,800	8		18,200	13		31,200
4		10,400	9		20,800	14		33,800
5		13,000	10		23,400	15		36,400

16		39,000	27		65,000	38		91,000
17	X	39,000	28		67,600	39		93,600
18		41,600	29		70,200	40		96,200
19		44,200	30		72,800	41		98,800
20		46,800	31		75,400	42		101,400
21		49,400	32		78,000	43		104,000
22		52,000	33		80,600	44		106,600
23		54,600	34		83,200	45		109,200
24		57,200	35	X	83,200	46		111,800
25		59,800	36		85,800			
26		62,400	37		88,400			

Andy is now done in Week 46—that small adjustment shaved three weeks off his deadline! Now, if you simply commanded any writer to write his or her book a month faster, that would be likely to induce hysteria. But add 50 words to a chunk? That's a goal most writers can embrace with very little stress.

What about taking it a step further and adding 100 words to Andy's chunk?

Week		Cum. Words	Week		Cum. Words	Week		Cum. Words
1		2,800	11		28,000	21		53,200
2		5,600	12		30,800	22		56,000
3		8,400	13		33,600	23		58,800
4		11,200	14		36,400	24		61,600
5		14,000	15		39,200	25		64,400
6	X	14,000	16		42,000	26		67,200
7		16,800	17	X	42,000	27		70,000
8		19,600	18		44,800	28		72,800
9		22,400	19		47,600	29		75,600
10		25,200	20		50,400	30		78,400

31		81,200	36		92,400	41		106,400
32		84,000	37		95,200	42		109,200
33		86,800	38		98,000	43		112,000
34		89,600	39		100,800			
35	X	89,600	40		103,600			

The results have Andy meeting his deadline in week 43. He has shaved 6 whole weeks—a month and a half!—off his originally projected deadline. That's a powerful equation.

I have found it's difficult to adjust any writer's chunk by more than 100 words at a time. A writer's chunk is a consistent thing, limited in its elasticity. That's not to say that you may have one of those magic writing days where the words gush out and you look up to discover fifteen pages have appeared—that does happen. Just not consistently, so its unwise to count on such a streak saving you from your looming deadline. Working within your chunk ensures your best work in consistent production.

If you have to step it up considerably, however, the single most effective tactic you can take is to add another chunk to your week. If we shift Andy's schedule from four to five chunks per week, watch what happens:

Week		Cum. Words	Week		Cum. Words	Week		Cum. Words
1		3,000	12		33,000	23		63,000
2		6,000	13		36,000	24		66,000
3		9,000	14		39,000	25		69,000
4		12,000	15		42,000	26		72,000
5		15,000	16		45,000	27		75,000
6	X	15,000	17	X	45,000	28		78,000
7		18,000	18		48,000	29		81,000
8		21,000	19		51,000	30		84,000
9		24,000	20		54,000	31		87,000
10		27,000	21		57,000	32		90,000
11		30,000	22		60,000	33		93,000

34		96,000	37		102,000	40		111,000
35	X	96,000	38		105,000			
36		99,000	39		108,000			

Remember, here we've not expanded his existing chunk of 600 words at all, only added a fifth writing session. That single act shaved *nine weeks*—more than two months—off his original deadline. Faced with such a demand to write a book two months faster, many of us would default to trying to write more every time we sat down to write. The mathematical truth of the Chunky Method shows us, however, that the most effective tactic is to *increase the number of times we sit down to write*. That's a specific, actionable step rather than a generalized goal, and it makes such a huge difference. There's power in that math, not just in our words.

No doubt about it, the Chunky Method writing plan will help you step up your productivity to reach your long-term goals. But what about the day-to-day work of getting tasks done? Now that you know what to do, how do you find a way to do it? The secret is in the

Chunky Method list, and the next chapter will show you how.

CHAPTER FOUR: THE CHUNKY
METHOD LIST

Oh, if only life would just leave us alone so we could write!

There isn't a writer in the world who hasn't, from time to time, resented the intrusion of the real world. That pesky place where rent needs to be paid, children must be fed, houses cleaned, etc. Even those of us fortunate enough to write full time are bombarded with writing-related tasks that don't involve the process of getting words down on the page.

That's because in today's market, writers don't just write anymore. The days when a writer could grind out the great American novel in solitude and then leave it to a publisher to make him a star are pretty much over. Sure, writing will always be the most important part of the job—but these days, it's just that—*part* of the job. In truth, writers are now much more like entrepreneurs than artists.

Writers need time to research. Research is almost as much of a time-honored need and distraction as housecleaning. Nowadays, the internet offers a happy, immediate feast to the ravenous research beast—which makes the easy accessibility of information more of a double-edged sword than ever. Even fiction writers must devote time to quality research. If you're like me, you need to do actual feet-on-the-ground location research, not just the nose-in-the-book variety. Research takes time, expenses, and energy. Even fantasy writers, who get to make up their own facts and worlds, need time, thought, and documentation to build a consistent, viable world their readers will believe.

Don't forget the other writing related tasks, including editing and revisions. The tedious, nerve-wracking task of proofing galleys. Proposals for new works need to be crafted so that your career can continue beyond the present book. And if you are taking the self-publication route, there are a myriad of formatting,

, submission, graphics, and meta-data
˄sider.

˄nd then there's publicity. Many of us may never be lucky enough to garner the attention of a publisher's staff publicist. In fact, many writers go without any outside public relations support whatsoever, with the burden of getting the word out about their splendid novel falling squarely—and solely—on their own shoulders.

Couple all this with the reality that most artistic personalities tend towards, um...disorganization, and you see a real problem arise. It's rare to find an artist who is also an administrator—yet that's exactly what today's publishing market requires.

All of the above only takes in the professional dynamic. What about the rest of your life? All that stuff that happens *off* the page? You may still need to tend to a rent-paying job. You need a clean place to live, food to eat, clothes to wear, insurance to keep you healthy, a balanced checkbook, and a host of other practicalities.

And then there are the real people in your life, the ones who want dinner served or laundry done or birthday presents bought or committees sat on or...well, you get the picture. Writing a book when that's all you have to do is one thing, but writing a book within the demands of a real life in the real world? That's another thing altogether.

Your Chunky Method writing plan may feel like it's under siege. Lucky for you, you have a powerful ally in this battle: the Chunky Method list.

Chunky Method lists are champions of the artistic pursuit. You won't have to shed your creative self to get organized. In the same way your Chunky Method plan built you a path to your writing progress, Chunky Method lists can see you through the maze of demands on your daily time. Most of us know how to make a basic list. It's what you do with the data—and, surprisingly, what the data does for you—that makes the Chunky Method list valuable.

Research has proven that lists help our brain function. Pilots, surgeons, and others whose jobs must be done correctly and completely have relied on lists for years. Even household hint columns will tell you a trip to the grocery store is cheaper, faster, and more efficient with a list.

And maybe that's the struggle right there: it's a very old idea. It's so simple, we tend to think we can get by without it. And in many cases we can—but we'll only do that: get by. Once you recognize the power in making a list, it's harder to dismiss it as simplistic or unnecessary.

Lists do several things:

Lists create measurability. The very act of putting tasks down on paper makes them real and measurable. If you feel overwhelmed, the basic step of documenting your workload has been shown to reduce stress, because you are no longer asking your brain to hold all the data. The paper (or smartphone or tablet or computer) is holding it for you, and you can see the workload as a concrete whole rather than a storm of fuzzy individual demands. Lists don't forget. Writing every task down helps to ensure that no task is lost or forgotten.

Lists discount emotions. It's hard to argue or ignore a list. It's hard to tell a list you are too tired or would rather go play a video game. Once on paper, a task takes on the qualities of fact, which helps to pull it out of the emotional realm. You'll learn a little bit more about that useful dynamic later in this chapter.

Lists manage your muse. Just like writing down goals always aids in achieving them, getting your writing goals and tasks down on paper sends a command to your creative self that it's time to "get to it." It gives your muse marching orders, often well before you sit down in front of your manuscript. That's an advantage you can use.

Lists aid good decision-making. Seeing concrete evidence of your workload helps you make smart decisions about how to spend your time. For example: I have a friend who often calls me for last-minute lunches. Now, last-minute lunches are one of the great blessings of being self-employed and in charge of my day. That's not a license, however, to say "yes" to every invitation. If I've got a list in front of me, I might be able to see that "no" or "maybe if we can go on the late side," or "not today but on Wednesday" is the better answer to that day's alluring invitation. Questions like "Can I take on another project?" or "Should I accept the invitation to join this committee?" or "Can I hit the awesome sale at my favorite boutique?" could all be answered with more wisdom while consulting a To-Do list.

Simply put: Lists are smart.

While any old list is a good first step, there are many things you can do—and many lists you can use—to give your Chunky Method list more powers. Let's explore them one at a time.

First up: the fish.

ARE YOU A MARLIN OR A DORY?

Hand any person multiple tasks, and you will find out a lot about their personalities very quickly. Some of us tend to be the kind of people who determinedly hammer at a single, linear task batch until it surrenders. Others of us nimbly shift from one task to another depending on where we see possible progress. Attention spans come in short and long varieties. Patience comes in small, medium, large, and—rarely—extra large. Some of us are aware of our tendencies, and we know how we tackle complex or long-term challenges. Others of us aren't sure how it is that we get done what we get done.

I have found the clearest model for Chunky productivity was handed to us by the good folks at Disney/Pixar in the beloved film *Finding Nemo*. Ask anyone if he is more of a Marlin or a Dory, and he usually knows. That's the power of a brilliant story—we can easily see ourselves in the characters.

Marlin had one and only one goal in the film—finding his son Nemo. Nothing else mattered until that goal was met. All side tasks were distractions, irritations, and detours. Marlin saw his task as a one straight line in a single direction. Marlin is a get-r-done kind of fish. An activator. A goal-focused guy.

Dory, on the other hand, was always open to new adventures. Life was a series of multiple lines heading off in dozens of directions. Short term memory issues aside, Dory thrived on variety, was highly adaptable, and could dig joy out of anywhere. A *"just-keep-swimming"* encourager, a resilient adventurer, a happy wanderer.

Marlins are, for the most part, big chunk writers. They maintain a great deal of focus over a long period, they aren't fond of interruptions, and they are results oriented. Dorys, on the other hand, tend to be small chunk writers. They work best with a variety of tasks in front of them, interruptions don't derail them, and they love the process as much as the results (if not more). Many of us are a little bit of both, but most of us tend toward one type or the other.

What do these fishy archetypes have to do with to-do lists? They can guide you in how to batch your tasks. Marlins are going to want to get all of their writing tasks done in large batches—retreats, whole days devoted to writing, several hours locked away in their study, etc. Dorys are happiest if writing tasks come throughout their day or week—every morning before breakfast, in-between loads of laundry, on lunch and coffee breaks, etc. This knowledge helps you know how to fit your chunks into the many demands of your world. You'll really see the difference when we look at how organizing lists can work on a weekly and daily basis. The next sections will show you how.

THE WEEKLY LIST

I have found it tremendously useful to batch to-do tasks by week. If you are using a paper list, this is easily done with file folders marked Week 1, Week 2, etc., an accordion file, or even a file drawer with all 52 weeks in their own file.

If you prefer the digital method, weekly batching is easily accomplished by loading all the tasks for any given week on the Sunday of that week. That way you can divvy them up later when you begin your week (more on that will follow).

Why do this? The answer is simply that we wake up in different moods and facing different demands every morning. Waiting until the "day of" hands our emotions or our energy levels too much authority over our list. On a more practical note, some days allow for more productivity than others. Many writers I know have "in days" where they stay at home and get all the desk-based tasks done, while gathering all their chores and errands for "out days." You could see how that approach would be especially attractive to the big chunk writers among us.

When breaking a large task down into bite-sized pieces, weeks are a good planning mode because days can get a bit too detailed if handled all at once. And, if you've done your Chunky work, you know how many chunks you want to get in each week.

Most of us are facing tasks in multiple projects every week. For example, most of my weeks comprise tasks in these six areas:

Book 1 (the manuscript I'm actively drafting)
Book 2 (the manuscript in editing/proofreading mode)
Book 3 (the latest release out on the market)
Family & Household tasks
Social & Writing Group tasks
Church responsibilities

It's a rare week when I don't have something from each of these areas requiring my time. Naturally, priorities shift depending on who is sick, how close I am to deadline or book launch, if there's a holiday coming up, etc. Looking at the week as a whole helps to anticipate those priority shifts and adapt before it's 5pm on Friday and panic ensues.

As an exercise, open your calendar, planner, folder, smartphone, or your memory—depending on how you hold the work in your life—and fetch two sheets of paper. On the first page, list everything you know is on your docket for this week. You've now got the first building block for the list system that will give your week the

Chunky power it needs to get you up and running.

THE DAILY LIST

You've probably already guessed the next step. Divide Page 2 into 7 daily sections. Take those tasks from the first page and portion them out over the days of your week. Look at all seven days as workdays, or just schedule the Monday-Friday if you prefer. You could perhaps batch your household-ish tasks on the weekends while doing more work-oriented tasks during the week—do whatever feels most comfortable for you.

The important thing here is that *you* are in control of how it portions out, and you are looking just enough ahead to do some basic troubleshooting. For example, if you're packing for vacation on Thursday, it might be a good idea to schedule doing laundry on Wednesday. If your proposal is due Friday, it's much better to get started on Tuesday than Thursday. Most of us know this, but few of us let that knowledge truly work its way into our daily lives.

I do daily portioning every Sunday night, or Monday morning at the latest. I have found that I am too weary from the week to do it Friday for the next week, and if I delay it anywhere past

Monday morning, I'm too easily derailed by whatever lands in my inbox.

The best thing about this process is that you start each day with a list that fits *one day's work*. It isn't so large it chokes you, nor is it so small that you can't get in gear. A daily dose of Chunky productivity, if you will. If you've got a massive project due Friday, you will stress less knowing that just for today, you've only got a fixed amount of steps in that project to accomplish. Less stress means better work, nicer interactions, and lower blood pressure—everybody wins.

Marlins will probably be happiest batching all of their writing tasks for any given day together. Just like Marlin couldn't rest until he found Nemo, writer-Marlins won't feel settled until their writing tasks have been checked off. Ideally, batching means they won't have to get up in the middle of writing a chapter to take the car for an oil change, nor will they spend the time they should be writing a press release distracted by how their villain needs to get his come-uppance in Chapter 15.

Dorys are happiest if writing tasks are scattered throughout their day. If you are like me and don't sit still well for long, non-writing tasks interspersed with writing tasks don't feel like interruptions—they are much needed breaks.

Let's look at a practical example. Here is an actual to-do list from my day:

+ Draft blog post

* Get passport from safety deposit box

+ Process emails not yet entered in to-do lists

+ Send thank you note to reviewer

* Clean up the back yard

+ First chunk of 1000 words in current manuscript

+ Schedule tweets about book releasing next month

+ Download and task out edits for January book

* Check next month's birthdays and events

* Balance checkbook

+ Second chunk of 1000 words in current manuscript (see note)

* Grocery list

Note: Thanks to the wisdom of Chunky Method analysis, I've learned that the best way for me to reach 2000 words a day is to write in two 1,000 word chunks.

Those tasks marked with "+" are writing-related, while those marked with a "*" are not. You'll see that I take my list-making very seriously, recording all aspects of my life, right down to the grocery list. It is a standing joke in my house that if it is not on the list, it won't get done.

A Marlin's daily list of these same tasks might look like this:

* Check next month's birthdays and events
* Grocery list
+ First chunk of 1000 words in current manuscript
+ Schedule tweets about book releasing next month
+ Download and task out edits for January book
+ Draft blog post
+ Second chunk of 1000 words in current manuscript
+ Process emails not yet entered in to-do lists
+ Send thank you note to reviewer
* Get passport from safety deposit box
* Clean up the back yard
* Balance checkbook

The writing tasks are all in one nice block, giving our author an energizing sense of accomplishment when he or she gets to the end of that block. She won't spend her best energies on her grocery list, which could be done over breakfast coffee, nor will she end up grumbling as she cleans up the back yard because she just got a fabulous idea for how to end Chapter 4.

Dorys, on the other hand, will have a list of those same tasks that looks a bit different:

+ Process emails not yet entered in to-do lists

+ Send thank you note to reviewer

* Check next month's birthdays and events

+ First chunk of 1000 words in current manuscript

* Get passport from safety deposit box

+ Schedule tweets about book releasing next month

+ Download and task out edits for January book

* Grocery list

+ Second chunk of 1000 words in current manuscript

* Clean up the back yard

+ Draft blog post

* Balance checkbook

In this case, desk-based tasks are book-ended by things that involve movement and interaction. The break a Dory needs after a high-intensity tasks becomes something else useful like making a grocery list—not defaulting to a zone-out chasing down internet cat videos. Dorys need variety in their day to recharge their focus, and this list capitalizes on that need rather than undermining it.

Just by implementing these simple strategies, you gain more control over the workflow of your day. There's one more tactic—a related skill that is perhaps the most essential of them all—to fire up your productivity.

THE MAGIC NUMBERS

Just having a list of things to do is a great start. In that single step, you've already given yourself a much greater shot at productivity and focus. Pat yourself on the back for embracing the Chunky Method of writing and look forward to great things.

But we're not done.

The secret to really mastering that to-do list, to experiencing the power of the Chunky Method in your writing career, isn't in words at all. It's in numbers.

Simply put, the secret is this: a to-do list is good, but a numbered to-do list is awesome. Why? Because knowing what to do *next* is the most powerful thought of all. Numbering your list can not only help with setting priorities, but with creating a variety of tasks (writing/non-writing, active/inactive, high intensity/low intensity) to maximize your day.

You've already given your muse a daily focus in your list—your brain can relax and re-direct all those brain cells that would have been worrying about tomorrow to spend their gray matter on today. Now spend five minutes every morning ordering that to-do list, and you sharpen that focus even more. Numbering your daily list forces you to think about what *must* be done and compare that with what can get done *if you have time.* You'll develop an awareness of which projects to tackle first thing in the morning and which are better left until after lunch. When you finish #2 on your list, your subconscious has already settled itself on the fact that #3 is next, even if #3 doesn't sound like an enticing prospect. You'll be amazed at how this seemingly thin layer of accountability fires up your willpower.

Marlins, you've already learned that you like your writing tasks batched together. If you can't tackle them first, your brain can still relax knowing you've made a place for them later in the day. If you've put them all at the start of your day, imagine the resulting glow of accomplishment and how it will carry you through the rest of your waiting tasks. You are making your focus work for you, and setting a structure to keep those pesky interruptions at bay.

Dorys, a list that bounces back and forth between writing and other tasks is likely to keep you from dragging mid-day or getting distracted by something that shouldn't even be on your list for that day. Alternate sitting and moving tasks, or make sure you have a less intensive task in between two high intensity projects. Now instead of bemoaning what others mislabel as a lack of focus, you are harnessing your resilient ability to shift between diverse tasks. You are working *with* your strength instead of *against* it.

There are many productivity apps and softwares out there to help you build your list, but make sure whatever format you choose allows you to order tasks within a day. My personal favorite, *Things*, doesn't use numbers but lets you "stack" your tasks from top to bottom in the order you desire. Before I used *Things*, I simply looked at my list and wrote a corresponding number before each item. With a little experimentation, you will find the system that works for you.

No matter how you accomplish ordering your tasks, you will see a significant increase in what you get done each day. The power of focusing on "what's next"—and *only* on "what's next" (instead of two weeks away or a month from Thursday) —will yield amazing results in your days.

The key is this: You've changed the decision process in how you choose your next task. Now, you have allowed your logical mind to make that decision outside of the moment by ordering your tasks earlier in the day. When it comes time to tackle the next task, your emotional self—so easily dictated by hunger, annoyance, that last irritating phone call, or the sugar crash from today's vending-machine lunch—must *reject* that decision in order to do what it wants. That rejection is just a tiny bit harder than a simple choice, and that tiny bit is just enough edge to keep you on your productive path.

I know it sounds small, but it isn't. Give yourself the focus of a list, sharpen that focus by ordering that list according to your natural tendencies, and you will take great steps toward productivity. You are giving yourself the tools you need to get the job done in the time you have. Can a list really do all that? I believe it can. In fact, I believe an ordered list is the single most effective tactic to fitting all of your life—writing and otherwise—into the space of your days.

CHAPTER FIVE: CHUNKS IN HIDING—MUSE ON COMMAND

By now, you know what you ought to do. You have your Chunky Method plan laid out before you and it makes sense. You're game to try it on for size. You've made time for your chunk today, and you sit down at your keyboard (or notebook, tablet, or whatever), ready to "Get Chunky."

And nothing happens.

We've all been there—that horrid place where you hear the blinking cursor laughing at you or stare at the dreadful yawning gap of a blank page. You are all dressed up and ready to go, but your muse seems to have stood you up.

You realize your chunk for the precious asset it is, and you don't want to squander it playing Candy Crush or obsessing over your Amazon rankings (or lack thereof...). You need to get underway right away—but how?

Fret not, help is on the way. Here, to help you out, are my best tricks for jumpstarting a muse gone AWOL:

SENSORY TRIGGERS

Good, enthralling writing pulls us deeply into a scene. Both fiction and nonfiction need to have an engrossing element of storytelling in order to drive the point home. Sensory details are one of the most powerful ways to make that happen.

Pull up a separate document—I don't advise doing this within your manuscript or you're bound to end up with a Dickensonian-length description—and start describing the setting and characters of your current work with each of the five senses. Remember, you're essentially brainstorming—you won't use everything you write down, but write down everything that comes to mind.

Touch: What is your character touching? How does it feel? What is the temperature of the environment and how is that affecting your characters? What textures meet their fingers? Is there something they want to touch but can't? What are they sitting on, standing on, leaning up against, etc., and what does it feel like?

Hearing: What sounds command their attention? What's in the background? What do sounds or voices remind them of? How do the sounds fight or enhance the mood? Think in terms of both animate and inanimate objects.

Sight: What's the lighting? What can they see? What can't they see? Which details—hand gestures, raised eyebrows, rich fabrics, clothes worn thin—give them information or influence their emotions? Look around all four walls of the room or turn full circle if you are outdoors.

Smell: Studies show scent can be the most powerful influence on our emotions. What is strong in the air? Faint? Is it pleasant or offensive? Is there food nearby? Fire? Plants or flowers? Again, be sure to think of animate and inanimate objects.

Taste: Food comes to mind first, but we taste many other things that can enhance a scene so don't ignore this even if there's no food involved. Bile, blood, salt water, tears, a dry dusty mouth, fresh or stale water can all be tasted by your character and evoke a strong emotion.

The key here is to write up a document with an unedited collection of these observations. Force yourself to think beyond the obvious or to go for surprising combinations. For example, a character who smells apple pie baking in a frightening situation presents an intriguing dynamic to your reader.

Once you've filled your page—or even pages—go hunting. Pick the most powerful detail for each sense. Most times, less is more, and you're likely to know the "gems" when you see them. Go back and slip these into your scene and watch the vitality emerge.

Whether or not you're stuck, this is always a good tool for taking a bland scene to a higher level, or heightening crucial scenes in your plot.

WRITING EXERCISES AND TRICKS

There are bookshelves filled with writing exercises to jumpstart your muse, but here are a few of my favorites:

1. Write until you know what will happen next, then stop. This was a favorite of Ernest Hemingway, and one I find particularly useful for Chunky Method writers. If you end your chunk at a place where you know what happens next, you launch your brain into percolate mode until you sit down to write again. It means your next chunk will be itching to get down on paper when you sit down to work again, and that's a far more empowering feeling than the dread of facing the blank page. One word of caution: write yourself a note! More times than I can count I have left my desk, sure I couldn't possibly forget the stunning idea I had to continue the scene, only to return stumped and annoyed. Usually two or three words are all that's required.

2. Cast your book. Hit the internet or check out a dozen issues of *People* magazine from your local library (I have actually done this!) and look for the faces of your characters. I especially like celebrities because I can usually find multiple pictures, audio clips, video clips, and such. Not only does it help you to flesh out the character in your head, but it is useful information for the art department when designing your cover. Take care your character doesn't become an imitation of any one celebrity, but a face or body type can serve as a vital jumping off point for your own imagination.

3. Tidbit envelopes. In my office or kitchen at any given time are three manila envelopes: one for my current book, one for future books, and one for miscellaneous tidbits. Anytime I come across a detail such as a photo, magazine ad, shred of paper, feather, etc. that speaks to me about a particular project, I slip it into the envelope. The miscellaneous envelope is for anything that piques my interest, even if I have no idea what project it might involve. More than one of my books has been launched simply by browsing through these catch-alls. Of course, these days Pinterest or Evernote have become a digital version of this process, and I use them as well. Follow this simple rule: if it catches your eye—even if you can't explain why—stash it for future use.

4. Play "Extreme What If?" All writers play some version of "what if?" when they plot. What if she knows who is after her? What if he doesn't think she loves him? What if she knows they are lying to her? Take this useful tactic and push it a step further by forcing yourself to come up with not just one or two scenarios, but at least ten. Why? Because scenarios number one through five are likely to be sensible. Six or seven might push the boundaries. Nine and ten are going to be outrageous, and the seeds of the best ideas often come from outrageous or surprising notions. Some of my best plot twists have been born of crazy ideas that just needed a little tweaking to work.

5. Three random words. Take three random words and force yourself to write a short piece that connects them. Kids are champions at this: Ask the little people around you to give you three words, and you'll get some doozies that will require a whopping imagination to connect. If there are no kids around, open a magazine article, close your eyes, and point until you come up with three nouns, verbs, or adjectives. You might not come up with text that you can use in your current manuscript, but you just might get the juices flowing to move you past "stuck" mode.

6. Opposites attract. One of my favorite writing axioms is this: "A vice is a virtue taken two steps too far." That responsible hero in your book? What happens if you turn the threat level up on him? Will he become controlling? Overprotective? Conversely, the best, most interesting villains *think* what they're doing is right—or at least justifiable. What's behind that craving for world domination? Why is that woman so cruel? Take some time to explore the opposite of your character's main trait, and you'll discover depth and texture that will make him or her come truly alive and be more memorable for your readers.

CHAPTER SIX: WHY BOTHER?

In a perfect world, we would all be able to sashay up to our desks and produce consistent brilliance.

I don't live in a perfect world, and neither do you. Life is very skilled at taking our plans and twisting them into stress-producing knots. Expectations don't always meet with reality, and creativity is not an assembly-line pursuit.

It is, however, a worthy one. One worth doing well. One worth doing at a pace that can lead you to success.

A CHUNKY TRUTH: GOOD INTENTIONS ARE ALWAYS BOLSTERED BY BEST PRACTICES.

You've been given a gift and a desire and a talent, and those things should be honored. If you have the desire to write, it's worth the investment to learn the best ways to facilitate that desire. It is possible to just write when you feel like it, just how you feel like it, and meet with success—it's just not probable that doing so will keep you on schedule to meet your deadline.

Most of us don't have endless hours to devote to our writing. Our lives are just too full for that sort of isolated focus. Having a system in place ensures that the time you do devote to your writing yields the maximum results possible. By embracing the Chunky Method, you give yourself the gift of a structure designed to get all the way to "THE END." You gain information and strategies to help you adapt and improve what you are currently doing. If you want to *just play* at writing, any old way will do. But if you want to be serious and productive, getting Chunky is a good way (not the only way, mind you, but a good one) to step up your creative game.

A CHUNKY GOAL: CONTROL WHAT YOU CAN.

Writing is a two way street. Actually, I find it to be a 24-lane highway. An author not only needs readers, but designers, publishers, publicists, discoverability, technology, distribution…you get the picture. The truth is that once you've created the best product you can, you end up handing your baby off to myriad external factors beyond your influence. Publishing house budgets change. Someone else can produce a similar book and have it go straight to number one, leaving you slack-jawed in the shadows. Imprints close. Public appetites change. Editors get sacked. A hundred factors completely out of your control can affect your career.

But how you write, how consistently you write, and how dependable you are as a writer? These are the things *totally in your control.*

It's easy to get caught up in this year's latest success scheme, the social media platform of the day, or obsessing over reviews in the hopes that any of those will boost your career. It's not that they can't, but you don't have much of a say in whether or not they do. You have plenty of say—in fact, you have *all* of the say—in whether or not you make your next deadline. Isn't that where you want to spend your energy?

A CHUNKY CONCLUSION: THIS IS WHAT MAKES A PROFESSIONAL.

Yes, divas exist. People with so much talent it pretty much doesn't matter how they behave? Authors with so much star power that editors and agents and publicists bend over backwards to accommodate their idiosyncrasies and faults? It happens. This is one of those businesses where stunning sales cover a multitude of authorial sins.

Still, that's not the wisest of career plans. Sales and fame are fickle things, and if a diva is only as good as her last bestseller, life is going to get pretty sticky if her sales go even a little bit south. Or a whole lot south. The publishing world is full of one- or three-hit wonders we never hear about anymore. It's a brutal world out there on the bookshelf battlefield.

On the other hand, an author who is dependable, easy to work with, and consistent will have much greater grace with his publishers. Even if you don't have a publisher to please, readers of independent releases aren't happy to know the book you projected for December is delayed until March because you didn't finish in time. Professionals not only behave professionally, but they get the job done. On time, and with quality work. Ask anyone in a creative field; the world is thick with talent, but skimpy on professionalism. Be the one who delivers, and you place yourself ahead.

With the Chunky Method, that's who you can be: someone who delivers. You've got the tools now. You have all you need to chart a path from where you are—no matter where you are—to typing "THE END." Start as small as you need to; even a chunk of 100 words can get you there, and the growth will come with time.

The key is to start. You've already joined the Chunky Nation, now go out and prove your citizenship! I'll be waiting to cheer you on at the finish line.

GET EVEN CHUNKIER!

GET A FREE GIFT
Click over to www.alliepleiter.com/contact and sign up for my e-newsletter—when you specify your interest in The Chunky Method, I'll send you the Chunky Method Writing Plan Calculator. It will do all the math for you as you identify your unique chunk and your path to finishing that book. For an even faster sign-up, pick up your cell phone right now and text the word CHUNKY to 22828. You'll be signed up in seconds.

JOIN THE NEW FACEBOOK PAGE
Get the latest chunky news, participate in polls, or share your tips with other Chunk Writers at facebook.com/ChunkyMethod/.

SHARE THE CHUNKY METHOD

I love to teach the Chunky Method. Contact me at allie@alliepleiter.com about bringing this powerful system to your conference, book fair, academic class, writers group, library, or community college. I have presentations available in live, webinar, and online class formats.

GET CHUNKY COACHING

Want individualized attention? Contact me at allie@alliepleiter.com about personalized coaching. Together we'll identify your chunk, craft a plan, create goals, and conduct a series of "check-in" sessions. If you're serious about getting that book written, together we can make it happen.

TELL ME YOUR SUCCESS STORIES!

I love to hear how The Chunky Method as helped you reach your writing goals! Here are all the ways you can reach me:

email: allie@alliepleiter.com
website: alliepleiter.com

Allie Pleiter
P.O. Box 7026
Villa Park, IL 60181

ABOUT THE AUTHOR

An avid knitter, BBC Television geek and French macaron enthusiast, Allie Pleiter writes both fiction and non-fiction. The enthusiastic but slightly untidy mother of two grown children, Allie spends her days working on an average of four books at a time, buying yarn, and finding new ways to avoid housework. Allie hails from Connecticut, moved to the midwest to attend Northwestern University, and currently lives outside Chicago, Illinois. The "dare from a friend" to begin writing has produced two parenting books and over twenty novels. In addition to various national presentations on The Chunky Method, Allie speaks on faith, women's issues, personal resilience, and writing craft. Visit her website at www.alliepleiter.com or her knitting blog at
www.DestiKNITions.blogspot.com

Made in the USA
Columbia, SC
25 March 2019